STARKEEPER

HOW TO SURVIVE WHEN SOCIETY LETS YOU DOWN

A Guidebook

How to Survive When Society Lets You Down

A Guidebook

Starkeeper Morton

ISBN 978-1-959555-78-0

Cover design & typesetting by riverdesignbooks.com

Published by Platypus Publishing

For anyone let down by Society. This is for *you*.

Inspired by the bravery of my daughter Poppy

Held by Scott, Lulu & Rosabelle,
who lived every word and were the real bearers of
endless cups of tea.

To Rachel, Natalija, Mandy, Caroline and Alison,
who didn't let us down.

CONTENTS

An Invitation from
the Heart

As you open this book, you open a door to a place where you are warmly welcomed. Thank you for coming. I have been dreaming of your arrival.

I am holding your hand as you read this book, and I am making endless cups of tea. You can trust that here, your experience matters; it has value. I am looking directly into your eyes, in the way that helps the heart listen, as I say, "I am sorry this has happened to you."

I acknowledge all the reasons that called you to open this book.

We lament as we watch the sun set on the world we find ourselves in, brush up against the stark contrast with the one we dream of. But here, together, we feel less alone. The presence of others, also feeling let down, encircles us.

Although darkness may seep in, together we light a candle. The magic of light is that it only needs the tiniest spark to dispel the dark.

We sit for however long it takes for the spark to catch.

We weep. We talk. We scream. We listen. We wait.

Somewhere, there is a sense of a sun rising, shining on our future selves. Where the time in which I am writing this book and you are reading it is all but a fading memory that feels like lifetimes ago.

Together, we awaken and leave, closing the door behind us.

Finally, like the patient moth seeking the light, we fly.

Keep dreaming,
Starkeeper Morton

THE BEGINNING: IF YOU CAN'T SIT AT THE TABLE, STAND ON IT

It is 1985. I am four years old at Renforth Yacht Club in New Brunswick, Canada. Somehow my mum has managed to persuade me to wear a frilly dress to a fancy function. The sort of dress that adults decide is beautiful on children but kids just find uncomfortable. I have to wear my black shiny, "snappy" shoes, as I call them. My blonde hair is brushed, and my blue eyes are surveying the scene of terror unfolding in front of me.

I may look like I fit in, like I am playing the role that I am dressed for, but a terrible injustice is taking place, and I have decided I am taking no part in it. ALL the boys are chasing ALL the girls in circles around the tables. The girls are screaming, and the parents, despite numerous attempts, have been unable to manage the chaos.

There comes a time for us all where we simply have had enough and need to take control of a situation before it takes control of us. As a four-year-old girl, this was the first moment when I decided enough was enough.

Clearly, the adults needed some help.

I pulled out a chair and used it to step up onto the lacy white tablecloth with my snappy black shoes. I carefully navigated my way around the china teacups, sidestepped the glassware, and avoided clattering the silver or squashing the crustless sandwiches.

I stood in the middle of the table and yelled, "STOP RUNNING, AND THEY CAN'T CHASE YOU!" I pushed both of my hands out in front of me to give them a visual. The girls stopped running. The boys, momentarily stunned, stopped chasing. I seized this brief respite to offer my hand to the girls, to haul them up to stand on the table with me. Together we would be safe on this tabletop fortress.

Of course, as an adult now, I don't recall any of this, but the story has been shared many times by my mother and others who were there. It has become part of my personal history and early identity, preserved in family folklore.

Perhaps a subconscious memory of this still percolates and it is why, as a teenager in Australia, I spent my lunchtimes writing letters for Amnesty International, campaigning for those on death row, and then later on, as an adult, I had a death row pen pal. It may explain why I volunteered as a yoga teacher at a maximum-security prison in Canada and later founded a not-for-profit community organisation in Scotland. I swapped standing on the table to sitting at the table with politicians in Edinburgh, telling them how their policies are only as strong as their ability to implement them. When the politicians didn't take any action, I gave a speech at the Public Policy Exchange in London.

Our early experiences in Society form how we show up in it later on.

INTRODUCTION

Friday the thirteenth is an ill-omened day for our eldest daughter. That was the day that she went to school a happy, healthy ten-year-old and came home a ghost of herself. I didn't even recognise her on the playground when I went to pick her up from school. For weeks, she was unable to speak, eat, sleep, or even change her clothes. Every day since then, we have lived through the experience of Society letting us down. The way we view and live in the world has changed forever.

I want to be upfront: this book isn't about what happened to us. That is not my story to tell; it is my daughter's. Something happened to her, and as a consequence, it happened to our family. We have decided, as a family, to not share the details about why Society let us down, a boundary set by our daughter that we will honour. This will probably annoy you at some point, that we made the decision not to share our family's story. You may curse my name, throw the book, or even stop reading it completely. One day my daughter may choose to share her story, but that will be on her terms and when she decides. In the meantime, I have her blessing to write this book.

What this book is about: how we navigated Society letting us down and what we learned through that process. I will share the learnings from our story, but not the details. Occasionally, I may give examples from other aspects of my life to offer clarity.

This is not the book I wanted to write, it is the one I needed to write. It is the book that I desperately needed when I realised that everything I thought I knew about Society was wrong. When we were in the throes of Society letting my family down, I felt I could make a difference. Change things. That our situation was different. I was certain that if I could get the right information into the hands of the right people, they would make wise decisions. The more days that passed, and the further down the path we ventured, the more we could identify the warning signs and patterns that others had forewarned us about — a collective foretelling. All the signs and omens were there and I, blissfully ignorant, missed them all. I was naive. I find it hard to forgive the person I was back then. This book is a penance for my naivety and to help anyone who finds themselves let down by society, to offer hopefulness in keeping the faith, moving forward despite the obstacles, finding a place, a way, to be heard.

In the early days of Society letting our family down, a friend gave me some sage advice. She said, 'Don't bother trying to change anything, you will drive yourself crazy.' She ended up being absolutely right. Her wisdom came from a well-intentioned heart that had also been let down. For that, I forgive her as now, retrospectively, I understand. At the time, I seriously reflected on her advice and had one life-changing insight: yes there is a high likelihood I would drive myself crazy trying to change things, but I would also drive myself crazy doing nothing. Either way, it seemed we were doomed.

Once I realised that Society had, indeed, let my family down, it opened my eyes, and I was able to unearth patterns of shared experience. It is always risky making sweeping generalisations, but since a great deal of people are being predictably let down by Society, there may be even more risk in not documenting that. I do not want to assume that everyone's experience has been traumatic; however, I do observe that collective trauma gets divided into different categories, and the impact is not collated as a whole. The stories may differ, but the endings are the same.

My intention with this book, then, is to compile and

share all the things everyone had forewarned me about, and that I experienced to be true, so that you can be wiser than I was. Reflecting questions and potential actions you may take are offered with the intention that you will feel more confident and supported in how to prepare, protect and position yourself, regardless of the nature of your Quest. I will share insights that were useful to me and in hope that they will be worthwhile for you too.

Part 1

I am not afraid of storms, for I am learning how to sail my ship.

— **Louisa May Alcott,** *Little Women*

Prepare

verb

to make or get something or someone ready for something that will happen in the future

Chapter 1

What Does 'Society' Mean?

I do not like the world as it is; so I am trying to make it a little more as I want it.

— **Helen Keller**

Society

noun

a large group of people who live together in an organised way, making decisions about how to do things and sharing the work that needs to be done. All the people in a country, or in several similar countries, can be referred to as a Society

Assumptions

I have made a terrible assumption. I assume that every-one has been let down by Society. After careful research and contemplation, I still hold that assumption.

My suspicions were confirmed when I was telling people the title for my book: everyone knew exactly what I meant without any need for further explana-tion. A few people asked for clarity on what I meant by 'Society,' but part of the experiment was to gain insight into how we each define 'Society.' I was taken aback by the response.

My friends who I believed had been most let down by Society, such as refugees, war survivors and health-care professionals, said they had not been let down by Society.

I am beyond curious about this response. I reflect on past conversations with my healthcare professional friends who took early retirement or left the health-care service because they felt it was failing them and their patients. I recall the war stories of my friend, which are full of resilience and bravery and how she overcame her family having to flee and nearly die. How can these people possibly state they do not feel let down by Society, when I feel let down by Society from my experiences?

From this I reflect on three possibilities. First, there

is a lack of basic awareness that Society has let them down. Second, there is shame around stating that one has been let down by Society, and it feels like a vulnerable claim to make. Third, there is a problematic issue with the definition of Society.

We Can't Challenge What We Can't Define

The fact that we all know the word 'Society' and belong to Society, but none of us agree upon a definition of it, is in itself an argument that we have been let down by Society. I even asked my friend who is a sociologist, currently studying for her PhD, for a definition. This was her offering: 'Society is like people and their relationships with one another. It's like a community but on a larger scale, for example *Western Society*.' The one common thread is that Society is made up of people.

What we can conclude from this is Society has let us down because people have let us down. We have let ourselves down, for we are Society.

Ultimately, I can't find a definition of Society that can help us move forward in a way that I am content with, but I can think of an analogy that may help. Think of a game. Any game. It could be a sporting game or a board game. The only way the game can be played is that everyone agrees to the rules. You haven't created this game or had a say in the rules, but you are bound by them if you want a place at the table. Now, as you start playing, it becomes clear that someone has not properly explained the rules to you; or everyone is not playing fairly, perhaps they are cheating; or the person overseeing the game is getting a little bit on the side; or it becomes evident they have big plans to be the Game Master. It could be that everyone else is having the best time of their life and you find it all a bit overwhelming and traumatising, but you are absolutely trapped in this game. If you felt like that at any stage, Society has let you down.

Here is a list of the types of rules you have inherited by being born into Society:

- Political
- Economical
- Religious
- Cultural
- Legal
- Medical
- Educational

Within these wider societal structures we also have smaller ones like our family, friends, communities and places of work.

What coheres a Society is understanding that list of

collectively held rules on how we should behave toward each other will be adhered to. It's following the rules, not simply knowing them, that forms societal expectations. We feel let down by Society when the actual behaviour toward us does not follow the rules.

I am from Here Too

I am with my family, at the Fireballs, the annual 'Hogmanay', New Year's Eve celebration in the seaside village in Scotland, where I live. People come from all over the world to see this spectacular event. Everyone is squished together down at the old harbour to watch. This mediaeval ritual involves swinging flaming balls of fire over the heads of local people parading up and down the high street and then ceremoniously hurling the fireballs into the harbour. Having young children, we arrive early to ensure everyone has a view and to soak in the festive atmosphere.

'I wish I had a pin to poke into her', I hear the elderly Scottish lady say as she squeezes up behind me. I decide to take the high road and ignore her. She arrived late and is clearly disappointed that she can't see.

Suddenly, I lose my footing as I am shoved into the wall of people in front of me. Worried for the younger children in the crowd, I brace myself. I whirl around to face the elderly woman who points to the man I had been standing alongside, peacefully, for the past few hours before her arrival.

'It was him', she accuses before I can even speak.

The man and I exchange a look and have an unspoken conversation where we come to the mutual understanding that what the elderly Scottish woman said was untrue.

'I find that hard to believe, given we have been waiting patiently for hours with no problem', I reply.

'But I am FROM here', she retorts. I realise, because of my accent, that she has made an assumption that I am a tourist here for the celebrations and not a resident like herself.

'I am FROM here too', I reply loudly. A hush settles over the crowd around us. 'I also heard you wanted to poke me with a pin. You are surrounded by foreigners and this xenophobic behaviour will not be tolerated'.

Perhaps she either did not know what xenophobic meant or could not understand my Australian accent. Either way, she looked stunned. What she did understand was that I was going to hold her accountable, with witnesses, and that the crowd was starting to turn in my favour. I went to speak to her again but my brother, who was visiting from Canada, stopped me. He has always been kinder than me and recognises when I am warming up for a rant.

The Scottish woman's experience of Society was that since she grew up in the town she was entitled to show up late, have the best view, shove people in the crowd, threaten them and make foreigners feel unwelcome. My version of Society was that everyone should be able to see, especially those who made an effort to come early, everyone should be safe, especially young children, and everyone is welcome to have a good time. What we had exchanged was cultural differences.

My local friends tell me that the only reason I can do, and say, the things I do is that I am not from North East Scotland. Perhaps they are right. I was born in Canada. I grew up in Australia. My natural default position is to be confident, assume everything is possible and can be done. I am always looking for ways to make things happen rather than all the reasons why they can't. The cultures I was raised in were fairly empowering for me, and although far from perfect, having a voice was encouraged, even if it was challenging to those listening.

Cultural differences are important to take into consideration throughout this book. What is acceptable in one town, city and country may not be in others.

Society Is Not Broken

'Society is broken', is a common phrase pandered as an explanation or an excuse. I am guilty of saying this in the past, flippantly offering the comment as a source of collective comfort.

I wish I could recall exactly who first said to me that Society is not broken but perfectly designed to do what it is meant to do. Society keeps a select minority at the top benefiting from the suffering of the majority. For the most part, Society does this very efficiently and effectively without the majority knowing, noticing or protesting. With this strategy the majority are unaware of how complicit they are.

REFLECTING QUESTIONS

» What is your understanding of Society? How do you define Society?

» What expectations do you place on Society?

» What parts of Society do you actively participate in?

» What parts of Society do you feel have let you down?

» What do you find challenging about Society letting you down?

» What elements of being let down do you find don't affect you as much?

POTENTIAL ACTIONS

» Consider getting a journal to record your answers to the reflecting questions and to record your experiences of being let down by Society.

» Commit to a day and time to hold yourself accountable to reading this book. Schedule it in your calendar and maybe set alarms or reminders to support your future self.

Chapter 2

Prepare to Lose Everyone and Everything

Rock bottom became a solid foundation on which I rebuilt my life.

—J.K. Rowling

Everything

pronoun

1. all things
2. the current situation; life in general

Abandoned. Betrayed. Disappointed.

It was breathtaking how quickly the narrative changed around Society letting us down. At first, I was told I had underreacted, and that is why we were let down. Then the reason changed to I had overreacted and it was my fault. When that didn't work, Society changed track and began targeting my daughter for not being resilient enough. The victim blaming and shaming is alarmingly predictable.

What I learned through this process is that Society accuses and criticises you for the very things it is doing. It is an unconscious projection by Society. I was confused, abandoned, betrayed and disappointed in the lack of support.

When we were let down by Society, we felt so overwhelmed we didn't know where to begin. The usual starting point is to turn to family and friends. But we had vastly underestimated the collective trauma of how many people had been let down by Society. Unintentionally, by sharing our situation and asking for support, we had triggered their unresolved trauma of being let down by Society. We were left with a handful of trusted friends.

Some family and friends abandoned us clearly and graciously, simply stating, having lived through Society letting them down, they just didn't have the capacity to witness us being let down too. I appreciated their openness and self-awareness. We may not have fully understood, at that time, but we acknowledged the transparency.

If you ever find yourself in a position of being unable to support someone, it is much kinder to own it and be clear with them about it than to impart false hopes, empty promises and expectations. Don't walk away without any explanation.

Others just abandoned us and to this day have not spoken a word to us about it. I struggle the most with those who not only abandoned us but also actively created barriers to make our experience more difficult.

Secondary Trauma

No one talks about this part in the story — the secondary trauma when everyone you thought you could rely on abandons you. There is perpetual potential for re-traumatisation in every ordinary moment. To this day, my daughter cannot have anyone approach her from behind without it being potentially retriggering. What we failed to understand was all the trauma of Society letting us down in the aftermath of addressing it.

I remember when a classmate of one of my other daughters tragically passed away, the parent shared with me how people crossed the road to avoid them and remarked how deeply that had hurt. Very few people have the ability to walk with you emotionally. If you find those people, hold onto them.

Walk with Us, Not Away

We were very fortunate to have some friends that walked with us rather than away from us, and I dedicate this book to them. They are as loyal as they are clever, as brave as they are kind. Most of the learning in this book stems from their wisdom. It would have been helpful if they had written this book before I needed it, but then hindsight is so much clearer.

Saying to someone who needs help, "Call me if you need anything," is not really helping. It bypasses the ability to actually help them but makes you feel as though you have done so simply by offering. Truly helping people amounts to being present, caring through action, anticipating need, and then fulfilling that need within your own capacity.

I see this all the time in the community food larder I helped set up during the pandemic and which supports 1,500 people. Sometimes people who are in crisis do not have the capacity to know what they need. Those who need the most help quite often have not identified their need. With the person who is experiencing the crisis permission, the people offering help can identify the need and then support the person needing help in the process, enabling them to fully experience being assisted in a truly beneficial way.

I remember someone calling the larder during the pandemic because they had no food in the house. Although we do not routinely ask people questions, they needed the opportunity to tell their story, to be heard and share why they needed food. This time it was a young woman facing domestic violence. I assessed that visiting the community food larder during our regular opening hours might be a barrier for her, so I offered her options about how she might like to visit. She had genuine fears of encountering her violent partner so I drove her to the larder.

After being there ten minutes she had only taken a few items: toilet paper, sanitary products, and a few tins of soup. I could tell she wasn't in a position to be able to make decisions about what she needed and how to help herself to what was available on the shelves. I stepped in and casually asked if she liked pasta and it was in this manner we filled several bags to the brim with food.

The friends who walked with my family were able to identify what we needed and offered their talents, resources, and strength to help. At that early stage we didn't even know what help we needed. Helpful things people did to support us included:

- Editing and reading emails, letters, and documents we had prepared
- Sharing their contacts and networks
- Actively listening and responding
- Offering childcare
- Inviting us over for dinner when we were being socially isolated by the community
- Reaching out and asking us directly what was happening rather than drawing their own conclusions from gossip
- Being consistent
- Respecting confidentiality

If you can identify what you need, then ask people you trust to help.

Safe People

Sometimes safe people sneak up on you. I recall howling for hours on my neighbour's couch after a meeting at my daughter's school. I didn't intend to show up in that way, it just happened unexpectedly as my mind and body could finally be in a place to offload without judgement. I can't remember having done that before, or since. I am still grateful I was given that place to fall apart.

One of the unexpected silver linings when Society lets you down became apparent to us: we learned what friends and family we can lean on in a crisis. Interestingly, if you had asked me beforehand who would be able to walk with us, I would not have picked correctly. People may take you by surprise. Prior to this we had a wide social circle, and in hindsight I can see we spent a lot of time and energy on people who were not equally invested in nurturing the relationship. I am now much more discerning.

The relationship which suffered the most, however, was with my other two children. When one of your children isn't thriving, as a mother that becomes your main focus and it becomes all-consuming. The fact that I would have prioritised, advocated for, and supported my other two children in the same way, if the experience had happened to one of them, did not factor in emotionally for them. I actually lost a close friend because of this. Her opinion was I should abandon my other two children completely and focus solely on my traumatised daughter. My feeling was, and still is, I had to make decisions based on the family as a whole unit. I have to own my decisions and accept the consequences as it is ultimately me who has to live with the repercussions of them.

One relationship I am grateful for is that with my husband. He and I were in agreement on how to approach Society letting us down. We both accepted it and were both naive at first. He had a tendency to be more trusting than me; more measured, detail-oriented; and assuming the experts knew best. I put our daughter at the heart of all of our decision-making and was unrelenting in accepting anything but the very best outcome for her, and on behalf of all children, who have a right to feel safe. I did all the speaking and my husband did all the listening at meetings because that was playing to our strengths. I was the rallier and he was the reasoner. I tended to our daughter's trauma by seeking out the best therapy and support available, writing emails, and making phone calls. He made sure that dinner was on the table, the rent was paid, and the documentation was up to date. It was a united front in the truest sense, and we are stronger because of it.

I couldn't imagine what it would be like when Society lets you down and you are in a relationship with someone who wants to take a different approach or strategy. All I can offer here is to trust the process. When Society lets you down, it places an enormous amount of pressure on you, as well as everything and everyone around you. If there is not a solid enough foundation to take the pressure, then cracks begin to show quite quickly.

Multiple crises, retriggering, and secondary traumas may start appearing in every direction.

Once I realised when Society lets you down I could potentially lose everyone, it meant I was now prepared to lose everything. I don't mean to sound overdramatic. I don't mean that you will lose your house or all your possessions. Although I have witnessed situations where that was the case. Rather, I mean be prepared to lose the things that matter: like sleep, sanity, a sense of who you are, and your place in the world around you. I lost all those things. The self-doubt will be crippling. This isn't for the faint-hearted.

REFLECTING QUESTIONS

» Who are people in your life that show up for you?

» Do you show up for people in your life, or do you sometimes cross the street?

» Are there practical actions you can take with people in your life today to support them?

POTENTIAL ACTIONS

» Make a list of people that may be able to help you.

» Identify a small trusted group of people who you can rely on for support from the list above.

» Set strong boundaries at what support you need and communicate that clearly.

» Review boundaries regularly and support yourself by setting time frames to do that, by putting those in your calendar. What works at the beginning may be different at varying stages.

Chapter 3

Don't Ask for Help, Expecting Anyone to Help You

I don't want to be remembered as the girl who was shot.
I want to be remembered as the girl who stood up.

— **Malala Yousafzai**

Help
verb
to make it possible or easier for someone
to do something

You Are the Best and Only Real Advocate

No one else is better qualified to advocate for you than yourself. The result you achieve will be highly dependent on your advocacy skills and what outcome you decide is acceptable.

Of course, some people are unable to advocate for themselves directly, my daughter being one of them due to her age. There may be other barriers such as language, literacy, race, gender, and physical and technological ability. In these scenarios there are advocacy organisations that can step in to help. The quality and commitment of your advocate will be proportional to achieving the change you wish to see.

Citizens Advice Bureau, in the United Kingdom, are a good starting point for generalised help. Even though, ironically, in our situation, the Citizens Advice Bureau we contacted ended up giving us the wrong advice, I would still recommend reaching out as a potential starting point.

Ask for Help, Then Go Above

"Look for the helpers," is the urban myth that gets trotted out every time we witness a collective trauma, watching, yet again, some horrifying news story. We comfort children by saying, "Look for the helpers." What always strikes me is that it is generally the ordinary people doing the helping. I always prepare my children, when in crisis, to find a mum with kids rather than someone in uniform. When we watch TV, I always ask myself who is not helping and should be.

A friend said to me, "You ask for help, so you are denied it and then you can go above them." Prior to our experience of being let down by Society, I thought the way Society worked was if you had a problem you asked for help and you received help. Naive. As we went further down the societal rabbit hole, and I realised that you ask for help expecting no one to help you, I became more realistic. To reach the "top" where the real decision-makers and people of power are, we had to first be failed by every single organisation whose purpose is to "help" us.

To give you an indication of what to potentially expect I list, in order, the "help" we asked for from Society:

- School
- Doctor's surgery
- Police
- Head of Education
- Local government councillor
- National Children's Charity

- Parent Council
- Social work
- Educational psychologist
- Director of Education and Children Services
- Member of Scottish Parliament
- Formal complaint to local authority
- Citizens Advice Bureau
- Education Scotland
- Lawyer
- Cross-party group at Holyrood,
  Scottish government
- Minister of Education for Scotland
- Public Policy Exchange Westminster
- Ombudsman
- First Minister of Scotland
- Press

The process of moving through this list, from start to finish, was one year to eighteen months, depending on what you consider an end result. This isn't for the faint-hearted. We asked for help more than twenty times.

There are a couple of tips that were helpful in our situation, and perhaps, they may be helpful in planning your own advocacy approach.

Plan the Process

Early on, someone had suggested contacting our local government representative, a local councillor, who was newly elected and ended up unexpectedly being a mediator for us. This technically wasn't her role. We were both out of our depth, but personally I learned from her how to gracefully navigate crucial conversations at a high level. We wouldn't have been able to request successfully the meetings we did without her connections. She ended up playing an essential role, which made me realise how vital local government roles are in Society when represented well.

Another ally we connected with early on was our local Member of Scottish Parliament (MSP). Prior to Society letting us down, I had never considered connecting with government officials. It was helpful to connect with people whose role was to simply listen and try to help if they could. I don't feel our local MSP actually did anything practical to help us, not because they did not want to, but rather because they too are trapped in a powerless system. Our paths continue to cross in other areas of my life, and I feel reassured that the people in power, making decisions based on policies, know that Society let us down and keep this in mind.

Taking the legal route is often the first port of call.

I blame all the TV shows and movies for conditioning us. But there are many steps you can take before you reach out to a lawyer, and usually they will ask you to take those steps before they will take your case on.

Do your research thoroughly on a lawyer, when you are ready for one, preferably one with relevant expertise in the area which Society let you down. Most importantly, you want to work with a lawyer that Society pays attention to. Society generally has a libel budget specifically for this. You need to find a lawyer that has a track record of making Society financially compensate. Only then will Society pay attention to your lawyer.

There was no law to protect us, which in itself is another reason why Society let us down. It took a lot of sleuthing to find out exactly what type of lawyer we needed. If other people have been let down by Society, and legally, Society has been forced to compensate them for this, there may be non-disclosure clauses which prohibit them from sharing information with you — in particular which lawyer they engaged.

We were very fortunate with our lawyer, in that they recognised we would be unable to proceed further in a legal sense because no law or legal precedent existed. Our lawyer took a professional interest because of this fact. He guided us the whole way without ever charging us. He also advised we pursue the Ombudsman route.

Before Society let us down, I had never even

heard, let alone pronounce the word *Ombudsman*. An Ombudsman appoints an official to investigate a complaint against a company, or in our situation, a public authority. We had to fail at every complaints process first before we reached the point where we could present these failings to the Ombudsman. The Ombudsman then makes a decision on whether or not to proceed with an investigation. Until you get to this stage, it is an "*us versus them*" scenario. We were told repeatedly by Society that we had not been let down, policy and procedure had been followed, and there had been no failings.

I remember vividly the day when I held in my hand the envelope containing the verdict of the Ombudsman investigation. I did not know if I could be part of a Society that was okay with letting us down. When I opened the letter and discovered that our complaint had been upheld, that yes, Society was attempting to take accountability for letting us down, I wept. Our whole family held each other, relief, validation, and vindication all rolled into one. I find it reassuring that we are in a Society that has an Ombudsman. From here on, it was no longer disputable whether Society had let us down. It was no longer down to personal opinion; on the contrary, it was a fact.

Press outlets are more likely to want to listen to you at this stage as there is a verified investigation from a reputable source. Many people, in the heat of the moment, use social media to vent and overshare about what has happened and how it made them feel. Although it may be satisfying at the time, to do something practical that gets an immediate response, I would advise against this tack for these reasons:

- The people you need to help you will be less inclined to assist you if you go public too early.
- Many will be looking for evidence that confirms that you are unstable.
- It is not an effective way to seek or create change.
- It becomes "yesterday's news" very quickly and loses traction.

Hit the Pause Button

If you are unsure of what the right thing to do is, I would suggest hitting pause with either going for a walk or sleeping on it. I rarely acted without talking to a trusted friend first. Whatever impact you want to have will be proportional to the time and effort you invest. Aim to play the long game, as this is Society's strategy. Society tries to wear you down so you will give up. Going public too early shows your hand, a predictable move, and is what Society expects you to do.

Also consider what kind of publications you would be willing to be published in. The same level of research that goes into finding a lawyer, I would also recommend applying to which journalist you approach and where and how the story appears in the media.

The Importance of a Clear Intention

Be very clear on why you want to go to the media. For my family, we wanted to share our story specifically so any other family who was going through something similar felt less alone. Anyone reading the story can contact the journalist involved to reach out to you if required.

Most journalists will not show you the article prior to publication, yet the more creative and compassionate ones find a way to involve you without showing you directly. In our situation, the sensitive nature of what happened to our daughter, as well as her being ten years of age at the time, meant that our story was published under pseudonyms, different names to protect our identity.

We eventually became volunteer advocates for a national children's charity that my daughter and I remain involved with to this day. If raising awareness and sharing your story about how Society let you down is something you would like to be involved in, I would recommend this route. Having the backing of an organisation means you are less alone and have more support and resources. Organisations are also better connected and networked. Journalists requiring a specific source will reach out to these organisations requesting what they are looking for. In certain instances, the organisation will then contact myself, or my daughter, and ask if we are willing to talk to the journalist unofficially or officially in an interview.

We have been involved in documentaries and I have been asked to speak publicly at large events. In scenarios like this we are given a press handler and supported through the whole process. We have our travel expenses covered if required. We have travelled the country as a result and have raised awareness about how Society has let us down, often for people who are in positions of power to change it.

REFLECTING QUESTIONS

» What characteristics are you looking for in a person or organisation when asking for help?

» When has asking for help served you well?

» What does setting a clear intention look like for you?

POTENTIAL ACTIONS

» Consider making a list of organisations that may be able to help you.

» Arrange this list in order so you know the best strategy for maximum impact.

» Do some research to find the right people to approach, and do some soft inquiry to gauge whether or not they are willing to support you.

Chapter 4

ACCEPT THE QUEST — KNOWING YOU MIGHT FAIL

Next to trying and winning, the best thing is trying and failing.

— **Lucy Maud Montgomery,** *Anne of Green Gables*

Quest

noun

a long search for something that is difficult to find, or an attempt to achieve something difficult

The Vow

I desperately need an operation. It's November 2007, and my seven-week-old first baby and I are in hospital. Since I am postpartum, we are in the adult hospital rather than the maternity ward. A thoughtful nurse rolls a cot into the hospital room. Not that either my baby or I notice as we are both loopy on morphine — me for the pain and my baby from my affected breast milk. It was the only way I could manage feeding her. My husband was offshore and couldn't travel to the hospital as the whole coast of North East Scotland was covered in a thick sea fog the locals call 'haar'. I am completely alone and in too much pain to be aware that I should probably be scared too.

'We aren't responsible for your baby if anything happens while you go to the toilet, shower, leave her side, or if anyone comes to take her. If you can't find someone to look after her by morning we are calling social services to take her', the matron informs me. She turned to leave as quickly as she appeared. I remember this moment with exceptional clarity, given the haze of morphine through a portal of pain I was in. I remember making an internal vow: 'If I live through this the first thing I will do is write a complaint about you and if I do not make it, I will haunt you.'

The only people I knew locally were my husband's

work colleagues, but I did not know their phone numbers. I did have in my wallet a crumpled piece of paper with the phone number of an auxiliary nurse at the maternity hospital. She had given it to me when I was discharged. I was so pathetic when they finally kicked me out of the maternity hospital that the auxiliary nurse gave me her details in case I ever needed help.

I rang her and she came. I gave her my baby. I would have rather taken a chance on the kindness of an acquaintance than social services. I had the operation and returned home. I think it is an interesting insight that the matron was operating as per the hospital's rules while the auxiliary nurse was coming from a place of humanity.

I kept my vow. I wrote a complaint about my experience in the hospital and the behaviour of the matron. I received a reply but no apology. Apologies make you libel. I was too busy surviving as a new mum to be interested in a lawsuit. I wanted the matron to know how much she had let me down. I didn't feel any better for making the effort of writing a complaint. Certainly nothing changed as a result. I had accepted this Quest and had failed.

A Quest is more than a complaint, however. A Quest should have a sense of *gravitas*. Accepting a Quest is an attempt for societal change.

The Right to Feel Safe

Before you accept a Quest of challenging or changing anything around how Society let you down, consider whether you feel that one of your human rights has been violated.

As a guideline, my feeling is, if your situation includes anything that makes you or someone you are advocating for feel unsafe, you should consider accepting a Quest. As a guideline if one or more of the Human Rights Act 1998 is being violated it is worth considering. Human rights include:

- Right to life
- Freedom from torture and inhuman or degrading treatment
- Freedom from slavery and forced labour
- Right to liberty and security
- Right to a fair trial
- No punishment without law
- Respect for your private and family life, home and correspondence
- Freedom of thought, belief, and religion
- Freedom of expression
- Freedom of assembly and association
- Right to marry and start a family
- Protection from discrimination in respect of

these rights and freedoms
- Right to peaceful enjoyment of your property
- Right to education
- Right to participate in free elections

This is not an exhaustive list and just because your situation may not be listed, doesn't necessarily mean you should not consider a Quest.

For example, I would argue that the right to healthy and accessible food should be a basic human right. This may well be a simple professional interest since the community organisation I founded diversified into food poverty and food insecurity during the pandemic.

This information is based on the country where I currently live, Scotland, and where the majority of experiences I am sharing have taken place. I appreciate that the information may be different for you. I offer this only as inspiration to empower you to make your own decisions and be aware that just because the list of human rights may not include your situation, does not mean it should not be there or worthy of pursuing.

Being an Advocate

Despite us accepting a Quest on behalf of our daughter, she was not invited to be involved or allowed to attend the meetings where decisions about her were being made. We suggested that she write a letter that we could take to the meeting and read on her behalf. Elements of our daughter's letter said:

> In school we learn we have the right to feel safe. Why doesn't this apply to me? It just keeps happening. No one does anything big to make it stop.
>
> After it happened I felt like I was no one and had no purpose in life and that I wasn't meant to be in the world. I feel that it's all my fault that it happened, even though people say it's not. It's not fair that I am the one missing out on everything when I'm the one who did nothing wrong and I did the right thing.

This was a helpful task for several reasons. First, it gave my daughter the opportunity to work through what she was feeling and the result she wanted. Second, it became less about what we as parents were pursuing and more about us as advocates on our daughter's behalf.

If you are in an advocacy position it is vitally important to involve and include the person you are advocating for. This is not only for their benefit but also to protect yourself.

Prepare for and Expect the Worst

I suggest you contemplate two possible scenarios if you were to pursue a Quest. The best case and the worst case. Most likely you will end up with the worst case, but at the very least by thinking about it beforehand you won't be taken by surprise. Hopefully, you will end up somewhere in the middle. If you know you will not be at peace with the worst case scenario, then do not accept a Quest. It is not worth turning bitter and resentful over.

I often wonder, if I had actually listened to everyone's advice beforehand, if I had been less naive, if I still would have accepted our Quest.

You know that quote, "Prepare for the worst and hope for the best." Don't hope. When you feel let down by Society prepare for the worst and expect the worst. That way you won't be as disappointed.

In hindsight, I wish I had reached out to other people who may have gone through a similar scenario so I could learn from their experience. At the time that did not occur to me, but I pass it on for your learning. Doing so may also depend on how private or public your personal Quest is. Our Quest still had a stigma and shame surrounding it, which meant it would have been more challenging to find people that had similar experiences.

Sweeping Under the Carpet

The phrase frequently used in referring to our Quest was 'being swept under the carpet'. It became a phrase in the early 1900s based on ostensibly lazy house-maids who rather than bending down to deal with the dirt would simply hide it under the rug. When you are involved in scenarios that get pushed into the dark psyche of Society it does make it more challenging to clean up. I would recommend finding an advocacy organisation, quite often these are in the charitable sector and have specialised knowledge, and they can connect you with other people.

Holding Heavy Things Lightly

I remember when my daughter came home, after that fateful day, and she couldn't even speak about what had happened to her. This, in itself, was extremely alarm-ing to me. I made the suggestion for her to draw about it rather than speak. What she drew shocked me right in the heart and jolted me into action. I took the drawing to the police station the next day to show what we were facing as a family. I had the foresight to take a photo of the drawing so when it was taken into police evidence we still were able to access it.

It was this learning that gave me the idea to have our daughter work with a local art therapist while she was on the wait list for other therapy. Drawing, rather than speaking, allowed her to hold something heavy more lightly and for me to take something I was holding lightly, more heavily.

The Witch's Cackle

I have a peer mentor who leads a charitable organisation whose woodland centre was targeted with numerous arson attempts. She installed CCTV for security so a notification is sent to her phone to alert her to any activity. Being notified was a trigger for her because loud sounds took her back to moments when she was trying to put out the fire. She observed this response in herself and changed the notification sound to a witch's cackle. The sound still alarmed her but it also made her smile, allowing her to respond from a less anxious place. Making small changes can have a big impact on your ability to respond.

Heart over Mind

Holding heavy things lightly helps us carry them. Part of my work is facilitating, and holding, well-being workshops and training. One group, despite having extensive experience and commitment, had a tendency to skim across the surface. Carrying light things lightly isn't the same as holding heavy things lightly. I wanted to find a way for them to be able to go deeper and show up authentically for themselves and each other. I wanted to find a way for them to delve deep.

I have a friend, who was also part of this group, who has a Master of Science in Mindfulness. Her dissertation was about considering Lego as an exploration of the subconscious. Somehow the idea of using Lego as a way for the group to connect, in a playful way, came to me, and my friend agreed to facilitate. Our hope was that Lego could be used as a key to unlock the depths of self to be explored. Using Lego with this intention and proper facilitation allows the unseen to be seen.

My mindful friend told us that we learn more from the intelligence of the hand than we do from working with the mind. Or rather, the hand unlocks parts of the mind that the brain is unable to do by itself. What I believe is that the hand is directly connected to the heart. Maybe this is the reason why we wear a wedding ring on our hands. I've always maintained that heartfulness would be a better word for mindfulness.

The most challenging part was for people to look beyond the Lego pieces to see what else was possible. They would externalise, blaming the pieces or the process instead of focusing on their abilities as the creator of their Lego model. It takes a brave person in brave spaces to be able to gently navigate the group, until they can be able to see things from a different perspective. The conditions for this to happen are rare in our Society. We are not often given direct experiences to explore ourselves, and the type of Society we all yearn for suffers as a result.

My greatest insight from this process was how few of us really know who we truly are. Much of our life is spent becoming who Society told us we needed to be, for the benefit of Society. We sacrifice our true nature, our gifts, our purpose, and then wonder why there is something wrong with us. We wear masks not of our own design or making. We give our power away to Society and then question ourselves rather than societal conditioning. Perhaps this is why Society has such a powerful hold on us, it is leech-like, sucking the vitality out of us, when a functional Society should be one which supports us to step into the power of who we truly are.

Name the Mission

Even now, five years on, we still refer to our daughter's Quest as "The Incident" or "The Situation." Every time I refer to it that way, I feel guilty. It minimises and makes what was a traumatising time in my daughter's life easier for others to digest.

I remember when the realisation of us accepting our Quest sunk in. It felt vast and overwhelming. We called our Quest "Operation Piglet." It felt more manageable that way and made us feel we were doing something worthwhile. It was handy to have a secret code word, if required, in sensitive situations. It made our Quest feel lighter.

Very early on in our Quest my daughter told me I should write a letter to the First Minister of Scotland. I remember smiling at her innocence and explaining how the First Minister would be way too busy looking after the country to help us in this situation. There are lots of people in Society whose job it is to help us. I promised her not to worry; we wouldn't be let down. I was more naive than my daughter.

REFLECTING QUESTIONS

» What is the worst case scenario if you were to accept a Quest? Write down your thoughts.

» What is the best case scenario if you accept a Quest? Write down your thoughts.

» Who could you talk to who has already accepted a similar Quest?

POTENTIAL ACTIONS

» Read back your answers on the first two reflecting questions above and notice how each answer makes you feel.

» Take some time to talk to people who may have already accepted a similar Quest so you have an idea of what to expect.

» Consider whether you want to accept the Quest. If yes, choose a code name to honour the Quest.

Part 2

I am not fighting for my kingdom and wealth now. I am fighting as an ordinary person for my lost freedom, my bruised body, and my outraged daughters.

— **Boudica**

Protect

verb

to keep someone or something safe from injury, damage, or loss

Chapter 5

DOCUMENT EVERYTHING

But still, if it's true, how can it be a lie?

— **Astrid Lindgren,** *Pippi Longstocking*

Document

verb

to record the details of an event, a process, etc.

The Best Complainer

My dad is the best complainer I know, not about the unimportant, meaningless things like sending a meal back in a restaurant, but he's the sort of person who won't be taken for a fool. If he gets a bill that is a bit more than it should be without reasonable justification, he will write a letter to the head of that company with the full ferocity of a government tax investigator. You won't be surprised to learn that in his former life he was an accountant, an auditor to be exact.

When I was growing up, every now and then he would sit me down with a spreadsheet and go through how much I cost him. That may seem an unusual parenting technique; when I share this with people they are often shocked. The reality, though, is that the awareness he was trying to teach me stuck, because out of all my moments with him in my childhood, this is one I recall vividly. It taught me that everything has value, and I understood my self-worth in relation to it.

One summer in my mid-teens, my dad employed me to take an inventory of all our house contents and reconcile it against proof of purchase. Nearly a decade later my parents' brand new house burned to the ground and they lost nearly everything. My dad was able to provide the insurance company complete documentation of everything they owned. This is highly unusual, as an insurance company's strategy is to do a generalised payout rather than reimburse every penny. They take a gamble that people do not bother documenting everything. But then they hadn't met my dad.

The sharing above illustrates why I continue to document everything, although perhaps not to the extent my dad taught me. But when my daughter came home from school traumatised that day, something instinctual in me that same evening decided to print out the school's handbook from their website. Maybe at the time I was looking for guidance, answers for where to turn and who could help. Or maybe it was the years of training from my dad kicking in. In any case, when I returned to the school website a couple of weeks later to find that their handbook significantly altered from the one I had printed, I had proof of their original content.

The Gamble

Society takes a gamble that you will not document everything. That you will be so traumatised by being let down that your emotions will have you overreacting and you won't be able to provide any evidence, or proof, that it let you down.

The fact I had documented everything from the very beginning was the most crucial step we took. It is important not to document your opinions and feelings, that is what a diary or journal is for. No one is interested in your feelings or the emotional impact the let-down exacts, rather, the focus, for Society, becomes about liability and compensation — how much it will potentially cost and, more importantly, whether you can prove how you have been let down.

Document facts, times, dates, and names at the bare minimum. Try to always follow up a phone call with an email restating what was discussed. I found a tactic of my daughter's school was to do everything by phone in order to bypass this process of evidence. I would always ask the head teacher to follow up with an email of what was discussed. If my request was not met, I would write an email myself, summarising the conversation. This process created a vital communication trail of proof that proved most helpful to the investigation that took place later on.

One of the narratives Society was creating was that I was "crazy." Having not ruled out taking the legal route, I made an appointment with the local medical surgery. Once I had given them the summary of our Quest, the ensuing conversation went something like this:

'What is it I can help you with today'? the doctor inquired.

'I would like to know whether or not I am crazy as people are telling me I am', I replied.

'You seem to have given a solid summary of the situation, which would not be possible for someone deemed crazy', the doctor responded.

'So I am not crazy'? I asked again, just to make sure.

'No, my diagnosis is that you are not crazy, actually you seem to be coping exceedingly well given everything you have told me,' the doctor said.

'Thank you. Now if you could please write that down and ensure that is documented on my file in case I need it in court. Is it possible to have a copy of that'? I asked.

Society also takes a gamble that you will be so overwhelmed by the documentation that you will give up. Society intentionally makes a Quest complicated with endless challenges and barriers to wear you down. Society plays the long game so you need to be prepared to do so too.

Viral

While writing this book, a social media post naming the exact same people in Society that let us down has been going viral. The very same points I highlight in this chapter are being mentioned: the reluctance to take minutes of meetings or to have informal chats and then retracting what is said; a predictable internal "review" carried out where nothing is found at fault, then followed by an external review that finds they did nothing right. I cannot emphasise enough the importance of documenting everything because what matters to Society is only what you can prove.

I reached out to the parents on the viral video to see if I could offer support. I felt for them. I have been in that place of wanting to do the right thing. But like many parents I have spoken to before them, I can feel the emotional toll the experience takes. I gave them contact details to a few key people who I know would be able to help them; however, I doubt if it will be followed through by either key people or Society. Yet another casualty of Society letting us down.

End of the Road

When we had finally reached the end of the road for complaint procedures, and we could confidently state, and prove, Society had let us down, we had all the evidence to lodge a 10,000 word complaint with the local authority.

I have no doubt they opened that email, didn't bat an eye, and maybe even laughed. I am making an assumption here, but I base it on the head of education's response which said: "In reviewing the matter, I believe the school followed the correct procedures in relation to the incident."

This is what we expected them to say, but now we had it in writing and could escalate the complaint. Remember you don't ask for help expecting to get it — you ask for help so you are denied it and can go above them. I would also like to point out that the complaint we filed also referred to the head of education, which essentially means the people we were complaining about investigated themselves.

We submitted to the Ombudsman our 10,000 word complaint alongside all the other documentation proving where Society had let us down and the letter where Society said it hadn't. The Ombudsman agreed to take on our complaint.

It was time to stand on the table.

REFLECTING QUESTIONS

» Do you have a good track record for documenting things? If not, how can you grow this skill?

» Do you have any skilled complainers in your life that you can learn from?

POTENTIAL ACTIONS

» Even if you are undecided about whether to accept a Quest, begin collating and documenting everything so that it is there for you if you opt to accept a Quest.

» Make sure you have set up a good categorising system with lots of space — I was surprised by the amount of documentation we gathered quickly.

» Take your own minutes at meetings, even if someone else has been assigned.

» Keep paper and digital copies of everything.

» Remember you have a right to any reports or information pertaining to you. Consider researching this further. If it involves a public organisation, you can do a Freedom of Information request, free of charge, to retrieve information retrospectively, if you are in the UK.

Chapter 6

Don't Play by the Rules — They Don't

If I'd observed all the rules, I'd never have got anywhere.

— **Marilyn Monroe**

Rule

noun

an accepted principle or instruction that states the way things are or should be done and tells you what you are allowed or not allowed to do

Biggest Mistake

One of the biggest mistakes we made was assuming that everyone followed the rules. What we were dealing with was a major safeguarding issue at our daughter's school that went beyond just her experience. We were advised to let the Parent Council know since the head teacher was not following child protection policy and procedure, as later confirmed by the Ombudsman investigation. We made sure we fully understood the policy and procedure so we could clearly identify when it was not being followed. We requested that the head teacher call a meeting with the Parent Council, which they refused. The intention wasn't to discuss our situation as an isolated event but to bring attention to ongoing issues around safeguarding and communication, as was later confirmed through the Ombudsman findings.

When the head teacher refused to inform the Parent Council, I went directly to them instead. The Parent Council agreed there were some serious safeguarding concerns that needed addressing, and they agreed to a meeting. However, I couldn't attend this meeting since I was not a member of the Parent Council. Moreover, the head teacher refused to allow the meeting to take place and then disbanded the whole Parent Council as a result of trying to address a safeguarding concern at the school.

Now that I understand better that Society doesn't play by its own rules, what should have happened was all the parents on the council should have met in an *unofficial* capacity. They were only following the rules, though, while Society was operating above and beyond them. For every official meeting held it is important that you understand the decision being sought after has already been made beforehand. Any meeting at this level is purely pretence, for absolute show, to placate and appease those who have been let down by Society.

When the Parent Council was eventually recreated, I was elected. Partially to honour all the previous Parent Council members who stepped up and did the right thing when the school was in the wrong, but also because when it reconvened, the head teacher cherry-picked and elected parents and teachers who would act in their favour. At most of the meetings there were more teachers than parents, and it was unofficially dubbed the Head Teacher's Council.

This new "Parent" Council was then put through rigorous training because evidently the parents were "wrong" and needed to pay penance for not following the rules. Interestingly, once the Ombudsman investigation proved that the school was at fault for not following child protection policy and procedure, among other "significant failings," there was no training for the staff at the school.

At this point in our Quest my daughter had missed two months of school. Overall she would miss three months before she was able to safely return. We were desperate to have an external agency to assist us. We patiently waited for her absences to be flagged because we wanted to go to the tribunal to explain why she was not attending school. Our daughter's absences were never recorded correctly, so this never happened. Because the school did not follow their own rules, they marked our daughter's absences as "authorised" so that the relevant social services would not be alerted. Safeguarding measures can only be activated when those in charge of activating make a decision to do so.

My intention in sharing this aspect of our Quest with you is to illustrate how you should not assume that Society plays by the rules, and in certain situations you shouldn't either.

My Two Rules

I have two rules in the organisation I lead. First, as long as it is legal and we are insured, chances are it is a safe decision to make. If we make a mistake, we learn from it and take ownership and accountability. In the six years our organisation has been supporting our community, I haven't yet come across a situation where

I have regretted empowering and trusting people to make wise decisions.

Second, I have a mantra: "*ask for forgiveness, not permission*" — this has served us, and our community, well. Too often people wait for others to tell them what to do or give them validation to proceed. I witness people so frightened of doing the "wrong" thing that they do nothing at all, and miss the opportunity to do the right thing.

Predictable Ploys

We also discovered some common techniques used by Society when you start to hold it accountable for letting you down.

Minutes to meetings are often taken by someone nominated by Society, which allows them control over what to document. Often these minutes are not shared with you; rather, those minutes are used for their own internal purposes. We started taking our own minutes and sharing them externally with Society. Minutes to meetings are legally binding. This is why it is important there is mutual understanding and transparency about what is contained in these minutes to meetings. We discovered, retrospectively, minutes to meetings were changed to "discussion notes," as these are not legally binding. Ensure it is clarified, and documented, before a meeting about what will be recorded and how.

Another technique employed by Society is to change the location, date, or time of a meeting at the last minute without informing you. Ensure that this information is clearly in writing as to what the agreement is beforehand so that if required any unannounced changes can also be included in the complaint procedure.

Remember to make copies, both print and digital, of all documentation. You have a right to all information about you. Quite often we found that files regarding our daughter "went missing" and were not available to other agencies trying to assist us. Once again, make sure you show evidence and document this in the complaint procedure.

Throwing Under the Bus

As you get deeper into a Quest, and you begin backing Society into the corner of accountability, Society begins to close ranks. Eventually what you will find is that Society starts throwing each agency under the bus. Education will blame social work who will blame the police, and so on. Internally, those in lower ranks get sacrificed for those in higher ranks.

Society is structured in such a way that it is almost impossible to fire anyone. An ally I had inside of Society wisely predicted that what would happen is societal perpetrators would get promoted or moved to a different department or geographical area rather than be fired. This was exactly what happened. With no accountability, ownership, or learning from when a member of a Society is letting another member down, Society then goes and commits the same mistakes elsewhere.

When you get to this stage in a Quest, watch for this type of throwing-under-the-bus behaviour, and know that when those in power in Society start turning on each other rather than you, you are finally making progress.

Meeting People Where They Are

In well-being and leadership circles the phrase "meeting people where they are" is common. A lot of your success on a Quest will be having to meet Society where it is, and not where you wish it would be. For me, meeting the people in Society who were responsible for us being let down, where they were, was compromising too much of my personal values, truth, and integrity. This is where mediation can be a very powerful skill to tap into.

Finding the right mediator is like building a bridge and having a referee that has an awareness of the rules. We were really fortunate to have our local government councillor step into this role. Without her we would have never been heard, taken seriously, or even had a meeting. If you can't meet people where they are, find someone who can do it on your behalf. It is fine to meet people where they are, as long as it is not sacrificing where you are, who you are, and the direction you wish to go in.

REFLECTING QUESTIONS

» What is your relationship to making mistakes?

» Do you lean toward asking forgiveness or permission?

» Are you meeting people where they are?

POTENTIAL ACTIONS

» Try to anticipate what rules Society may be manipulating to its benefit and to the detriment of you and your Quest.

» Make sure you know your rights and rules so that Society knows that you are informed and willing to hold it accountable.

» There are official rules and unofficial real ways of doing things. Make sure you have done your research enabling you to come from a position of knowing the difference.

Chapter 7

FINDING THE GOOD ENEMY

A wise woman wishes to be no one's enemy; a wise woman refuses to be anyone's victim.

— **Maya Angelou**

Enemy

noun

a person who hates or opposes another person and tries to harm them or stop them from doing something

Moral Compass

Finding my Good Enemy was one of the most helpful pieces of advice I was given. An enemy is someone
who weakens or harms you, while a Good Enemy is
a constant reminder of your strength at how to be a
better person. A Good Enemy acts like a reverse moral
compass. My Good Enemies are some of my greatest
teachers as they regularly remind me of the person I
do not want to be and how I do not want to show up
in the world. I regularly keep my eye on them to keep
myself accountable.

Quite often a Good Enemy may have more in
common with you, a shared vision, but the way they
want to achieve that vision is completely different than
yours. Occasionally, you may cross paths and have to
battle. I notice that when I am taking the path of least
resistance I am often lowering myself to the Good
Enemy level. I regularly have to hold myself accountable, against my will, kicking and screaming, to the
high road.

Nameless and Faceless

Naming and knowing a Good Enemy is powerful in a
Society that wants to remain nameless and faceless. If

there was one identifiable villain, we could all unite together and bring them to justice. The challenge is that there is no one person to direct all this Questing energy toward, so ultimately it gets diluted with no real impact.

Remember Society is us; people make up Society. All the people who create Society are our partners, family, friends, neighbours, and colleagues. They are the teachers, lawyers, doctors, politicians, police officers, etcetera upholding these societal structures we all rely on.

Complicit

It can be extremely uncomfortable to realise that the very people we love and trust may be complicit in a Society that lets us down. The only aspects we have any control over are our own decisions and behaviour. If we hold ourselves accountable to a high degree of integrity it brings out that very quality into Society. This tactic exposes the Good Enemy for who they truly are.

Let me offer an example.

One of the signs that told us we were making progress on our Quest was the email etiquette. At the beginning of our Quest, emails would be written like this:

Dear Mrs Morton,
Insert minimising, victim shaming and blaming
and excuses.
Sincerely,
Society

Halfway through our Quest, emails would be written like this:

Mrs Morton,
Insert justification and defensiveness.
Society

Near the end of our Quest, emails would be written like this:

Bare minimum of information required.
No signature. No acknowledgement.

Eventually Society won't respond to emails at all. Take this as a good sign that you are getting somewhere that Society does not want you to go.

There is a massive difference between *acting* respectfully and politely because you are told to and *wanting* to behave that way from a place of authenticity.

Throughout the whole Quest, it was really important to us, as a family, to remain polite, respectful, and kind. We never raised our voices, became overly emotional or unreasonable. We were leading by example, for our daughter, at how to show up in the world when life gets hard. It was also easier to behave that way because we were in the role of advocating for our daughter as her parents.

I would imagine, if the trauma had happened directly to me, it would be more challenging to be present in this way.

Saboteur

In the organisation I run, we shine a light on hidden poverty and trauma in our community. The majority share our vision for a flourishing community where everyone feels supported and included. For a few, this is a very challenging concept and they have different ideas of what community means. We welcome differing opinions and ideas. Yet, a few spend a great deal of time and effort trying to actively sabotage the work we do. The more time they spend trying to prove that what we are doing is 'wrong' inadvertently has the opposite effect and proves how much we are actually doing right. By their sabotaging behaviour, they expose themselves for who they really are.

Try to not be disheartened when the saboteurs show up. If your intention is true, and the work is honest and from a place of integrity, there is nothing to hide or be worried about. It tells everyone more about themselves than you.

Integrity

When you know you are a good person and act with integrity, your behaviours don't change, and others' behaviour can't change or affect you. When you spot behaviour changes in the Good Enemy, when the facade is exposed, when meaningless social niceties no longer make an appearance, you know at the very least you are making an impact.

REFLECTING QUESTIONS

» Do you have any Good Enemies in your life?

» If so, what shared behaviours do you have with your Good Enemy?

» What does taking the high road feel and look like for you in your life?

POTENTIAL ACTIONS

» Find your Good Enemy.

» Identify what behaviours your Good Enemy displays that teach you about your own behaviour.

» Discover a way you can monitor your Good Enemy's behaviour as an accountability measure for your own behaviour.

Part 3

A clear and innocent conscience fears nothing.

— **Queen Elizabeth I**

Position

noun

the place where something or someone is, often in relation to other things

Chapter 8

FINDING YOUR PLACE

Nolite te bastardes carborundorum. Don't let the bastards grind you down.

— **Margaret Atwood,** *The Handmaid's Tale*

Place (DUTY)

noun

what a person should do or is allowed to do, especially according to the rules of Society

Axis Mundi

Things are going to get heavy and dark fast, and self-care is too light a touch of a New Age concept to give you what you will need in your Questing. Instead, I like the concept of the Latin term *axis mundi*, finding the centre of your universe, a place unique to you. It is about a safe place that you can go to find some respite. This isn't a physical place, although it could be. But it is somewhere that exists inside of you — a bit like your 'happy place', but more powerful. I have accessed it during meetings, waiting in queues, and when the patriarchy starts mansplaining at me.

Serious Business

Questing is serious, and takes an enormous amount of your energy and time. Some things will have to slide. I had to massively re-evaluate everything. One of the first things to go was cooking for the family. I simply didn't have the capacity for it anymore. Fortunately, my husband stepped into that role. I couldn't ring my in-laws every week, organise birthday gifts, attend any classes, or practise any hobbies. My other two daughters received less attention than they deserved. I was self-employed so I had more flexibility than most, but we lost income and relied more heavily on my husband's salary. How I felt at the time was: you were either with us or you had to get out of our way.

At the time we were first let down by Society, I was setting up a not-for-profit organisation in the community, where we as a family had experienced our daughter's trauma. My wish was to create what we desperately needed: a safe place, a sanctuary, where we could find moments of peace. My daughter would come and lay on the floor of the huge empty room, unable to do anything else at that stage but just be and breathe. I stripped away the old and painted the new on the walls surrounding us. It felt satisfying to do something practical, where I could see immediate change and results. If only our Quest had been that easy.

Safe Space

The ironic timing of setting up a safe space in the very community that had let us down had not escaped me. That knowledge is painted in every brush stroke that covers the walls, it is imbued into the very bones of the building.

Safe spaces are hard to find. Now, years on from when we created the organisation, people sometimes step through the threshold of the doorway for the first time and burst into tears. This response takes them by surprise, but not me. I understand. We aren't used to being held well in Society and when we enter into spaces that understand this, something deep inside of us wells up and overflows with relief.

Pacing

In 2010, I found myself back at a meditation retreat centre, nestled into a beautiful nook of Scotland. I am seeking solace in a safe space. Moments before leaving to drive to the retreat centre, I discovered I was pregnant for the third time in three years. I had had postnatal depression following a traumatic birth experience of my second child six months earlier, and I am not in a good place.

I was not there so much for the meditation as for the respite. Having someone else to cook, clean, and care for me, even in such minimal surroundings, was a welcome gift. My husband and I have a mutual understanding that I need this one week a year for my sanity, despite my challenges as a meditator.

At the centre on this occasion, a hermit came down from the hillside and gave us some teachings unexpectedly. I had not experienced this on past visits, although I had heard occasionally it happened. We meditate all together. Afterwards, I take the opportunity to ask the hermit, "How long did you practise meditation before you felt you could do it?"

His response was liberating for me, "Ten years." My apprehension was relinquished. I had been putting a self-imposed time frame on myself. Ever since that moment, I have been able to meditate.

Managing Expectations

I share this story in case you may find it helpful to understand the importance of realistic time frames to be able to pace yourself and manage your expectations. When you experience being let down by Society it can be devastating and all-consuming. There is a sense of urgency that Society just won't be able to match. Society has its own agenda and timing that it uses to its own advantage and self-serving purpose.

In the immediate few days of the aftermath of my daughter's trauma, we desperately sought the expertise required for her to be able to meet her basic needs once again. Society continued to let her down simply because she was not deemed the right age to receive help. She was falling through the cracks rapidly and we were trying to hold her until we could get her to the experts who could help her. At the tender age of ten years old our daughter was unable to access the support she needed. If she had been fourteen years old that would have been possible. If an adult had been involved in her trauma she would have been offered support. But since she was only ten there was no specialised support available to her.

The National Health Service had a six-month waiting list, and with our daughter being in such an acute state of crisis we had serious concerns that the trauma would have irrevocable consequences if we waited that long. We ended up contacting over fifty individual private psychological practitioners before we found one that was able and willing to work with a child of her age. We would have to wait six weeks, but at least it was something.

In terms of the time frame when Society let us down, the first six weeks were brutal, and you may find the same, especially if there is physical or psychological trauma that needs to be addressed. It took three months for us to make it liveable, eighteen months to get some basic closure, three years to recalibrate from it, and five years for us to move on.

As someone else who had also been let down by Society said to us, 'You never get over it but the best you can strive for is to come to peace with it'. Perhaps this is why those who don't believe in God begin praying, or try to find their version of it. If that isn't your thing, you can always approach people who do pray. It helps to call in the higher powers, whatever you believe them to be.

Guide

I would encourage you to find a Questing Guide, essentially someone who can be a role model that you can emulate, when you don't feel you are enough. A guide is someone who inspires you on your Quest, keeps you focused, and shows you a way to achieve your Quest on a deeper emotional level that speaks to your humanity. If you are a religious person this may be more accessible for you as there is a built-in belief system. If this concept is new to you, then it may be a bit more challenging.

For my daughter, her Questing Guide was the First Minister of Scotland Nicola Sturgeon. At the time of my daughter's trauma, she was learning about democracy in school. They set up mock political parties with slogans and organised a vote. This is why when we accepted our Quest my daughter's first suggestion was to write a letter to the First Minister of Scotland.

Fast forward eighteen months, and we were sitting in the office of the First Minister of Scotland. My daughter had written her a letter and she had been invited to her office. At this stage, my daughter had been let down by every adult in Society who was responsible for her safeguarding: her teacher, head teacher, educational psychologist, quality improvement officer, head of education, director of education, social worker, and police. Regardless of your personal politics, the fact that the First Minister personally opened her door when everyone else was slamming it in my daughter's face may help you understand why my daughter clung to her like a superhero. My daughter even named her cat Sturgeon.

My Questing Guide was my future self. I needed to know that everything I did, every decision I made, and every action I took I would be able to live with myself in the future without regret. My future self kept me very focused and accountable. I had an imaginary scenario in my head where one day, in the not-too-distant future, I might open a newspaper or see something on the television that resonated with our situation. I had to do everything in my power to know I had tried to prevent that from happening.

Our Questing Guides were comforting to us. Your Questing Guide should be someone you find motivating and inspirational, who can keep you on track like your grandmother or a historical figure. It may even be your cat! The most important element is that you are creative with your choice and it is meaningful to you.

Perspective

Having a healthy sense of perspective through your Quest is stabilising. Often when we are in survival flight or fight mode we catastrophize. Of course, a Quest needs all of our attention, that is what makes it worthy of Questing, but it must not tip into the obsessive, all-consuming, self-destructing mode.

When I talk about keeping your perspective, I don't mean comparative suffering. This is where we sometimes minimise our own experiences because they seem not "as bad" as what we perceive others are experiencing. Comparative suffering unintentionally creates a hierarchy where we start attributing permission to what we are 'allowed' to feel. This is not a helpful process, to ourselves, or to others, who are also experiencing challenging situations. We start using our minds to judge, rather than our hearts to heal ourselves and each other. Perspective is a different approach. It considers other ways of viewing or experiencing a situation. Perspective is the seed from which empathy grows. From here I bring it down to basics. My daughter and I were together and physically alive. From that foundation anything was possible.

What I found frustrating was that I could come from a place of compassion and understanding from Society's perspective, but this ability was not reciprocated.

Society seemed to have an inability to understand, or feel, how letting us down impacted us. From our perspective, something happened that impacted my daughter's right to feel safe and be educated. From Society's perspective was something happened that made it not liable, and consequently there was no impact and no further action was required.

Remember, ultimately Society only takes into consideration what costs them money, and feelings have no value.

The Middle Way

I have a mentor that talks a lot about the 'middle way'. The middle way values the importance of avoiding extremes in any situation. My mentor is a practising Buddhist, and a retired CEO turned author. One of the reasons why I appreciate him as a mentor is that he leads with compassion. When on a Quest, it is challenging to be kind and compassionate in approaching people who are letting you down in Society.

If I feel myself getting swept away emotionally with the feeling of 'us versus them', I use a loving kindness meditation. Essentially, it is repeating this mantra:

May I be safe.
May I be happy and healthy.
May I be free to grow old and wise.

Begin with saying it to yourself. Then say it while thinking of someone you love. Repeat it again thinking of someone you are indifferent about (this is often the most difficult as we are quick to make judgements about people). Last, say the mantra while holding someone in your mind that you find challenging.

I found this practise helped me to be more centred, to find my middle way, by keeping me connected to my humanity.

Compassionate Conversations

We were never able to have the conversations we needed throughout our Quest. The types of meetings Society offered were out of necessity rather than humanity. Society is of the mind rather than the heart. What we needed was to be seen, heard, and validated. What we received was defensiveness, judgement, and justification.

So instead I held those conversations in my imagination, appealing to Society's highest nature and potential. The purpose was to visualise a Society that would be able to support and give our family what we needed to feel seen, heard, and supported. Having these imaginary conversations made no real difference of course, except it allowed me to once again find the middle way. If your Quest is following the middle way, then you are heading in the right direction.

REFLECTING QUESTIONS

» How are you pacing yourself around the time frame of your Quest? Is it realistic?

» What safe spaces do you have?

» What do you need to let go of to create the time and energy you will need for your Quest?

POTENTIAL ACTIONS

» Find a Questing Guide to inspire you and find a way to integrate them into your life by asking these questions:

- What do they pay attention to?
- What is their mindset like?
- What drives them?
- What are their values?
- How do they show up?
- What behaviours would you notice?
- What can you learn from them?
- What would you see them do?

Chapter 9

KEEP THE FAITH

If the year is meditating a suitable gift,
I should like it to be the attitude
of my great-great-grandmother ...
— **Judith Wright,** *Request to a Year*

Faith

noun

a high degree of trust or confidence in
something or someone

The Raging Sea

I have this tacky plastic card that fits in my wallet, but I choose to keep it by my bedside. It used to belong to my great-grandmother, although I don't know who bought it for her or even how it came into her or my possession. Single-handedly it has given me the greatest comfort in the darkest times. It says:

> Faith gives us an anchor in a raging sea.
> Calm in the midst of chaos.
> Vision to know right from wrong,
> and the courage to express it.

Dark Night

Any Quest includes an element of sacrifice. You will reach a point where perhaps what you are doing costs too much physically, emotionally, and/or psychologically. Some people refer to this as a 'dark night of the soul', but I was taught, and believe, that the soul is pure and full of light. I prefer to say that it is a dark night of the ego. There is Ego with a capital *E* to differentiate between ego. There is a healthy ego and then there is Ego that demands to be capitalised and command all the attention.

For me, I had a dark night of the ego early on. It was two o'clock in the morning about three weeks since we accepted our Quest. I couldn't sleep because of the thoughts turning through my mind. Everyone else in Society seemed okay with what was happening to my family so maybe I was the crazy one? I ended up calling an all-night helpline, one specifically for concerns with children. I shared with them our situation and they were so horrified, they quickly arranged a call first thing on Monday morning. I could sleep after that and didn't feel so alone. We still volunteer as advocates for that children's national organisation to this day because of that late-night intervention. When people genuinely care enough to help you, it is something you never forget.

Career Institutionalists

Career institutionalists are only interested in upholding the societal systems for their own personal benefit instead of supporting anyone let down by Society. Their sole ambition tends to be a steady income, a good pension, and possibly, if they are lucky, an early redundancy and retirement. Their very careers depend on the multi-agency interdependence working efficiently to strengthen and protect itself, rather than protecting those let down by Society.

Career institutionalists will defend and protect their positions by sacrificing their humanity and yours in the process. They would have files upon files of paperwork full of tick boxes, minutes to meetings, procedures and processes to legitimise and justify doing so. To them that is all that matters.

No one is born a career institutionalist. They are groomed by Society. It does not mean that a career institutionalist does not want to help but that they are absolutely powerless to do so. Over time, that lack of empowerment comes at a cost, and I imagine to be in a position where you are perpetually letting people down, you would have to become desensitised, discon-nected from it to be able to survive.

Above My Pay Grade

A clear sign that I was in the presence of a career insti-tutionalist in Society was when they responded to any request with the phrase, 'above my pay grade'. They completely absolved themselves of any responsibility by claiming they were not paid enough to care or help us. The response is often accompanied by a shoulder shrug, a slightly awkward chuckle, or worse, a matter-of-fact flinging up of the hands.

Some people may be totally inflexible and only keep to what is written on their job contract. Others may have really clear defined boundaries around what is, or isn't, their responsibility. The issue is the way a career institutionalist communicates and responds to an enquiry. If someone is turning to you for assistance, to make a request, or seek an answer to a question and you are unable to act, then at the very least, find a kind way to respond.

I am unsure if this is a local phrase, or if there are similar sayings in other areas. Regardless of how widespread the language, the message is totally unacceptable. If a career institutionalist feels so disconnected from their humanity that they don't want to help another being unless they are paid to do so, then at the very least they can connect the person inquiring to someone else who can help.

Why Signposting Does Not Work

Often if someone feels it is not their responsibility to help or they are not qualified or generally unable to help you as the one being let down by Society, a common tactic is signposting. This generally means referring you to another person, organisation, or societal structure better resourced to help. What I have noticed with the signposting process, however, is that it only works as well as the ability and capacity of the organisation you are signposted to.

The benefit of a sign depends on your ability to be able to first find the sign, second read it, and then last your willingness to follow the sign. The sign also needs to be pointing you in the direction you are wanting to go, and not necessarily redirecting you to the way Society wishes you to go.

What I have experienced working alongside many societal structures and other organisations, is waking up daily to an inbox full of meaningless and ineffectual emails that have been forwarded to me as part of the signposting process. There has been no effort in building trust and relationships, which are essential for me to have the confidence in signposting people to the optimal information.

I need to know that what I am signposting to is not going to make them feel more lost, because that will potentially affect the trust they have in my relationship with them. It is not a tick box exercise for me of simply forwarding an email and thinking my job is done. When people are taking their first tentative steps down an unknown path, it is helpful to offer your hand and walk with them for a while till they know they are heading in a direction they wish to travel.

When we were on our Quest, we were signposted to over twenty different organisations. The Citizens Advice Bureau ironically gave us the wrong advice. There was no follow up, no hand-holding, and most importantly no opportunity for feedback. They simply didn't want to know. It was a matter of answering the phone, ticking the signposting box, and moving on to the query. As an organisation, they purposefully ensure you do not have the consistency of the same adviser in order to avoid relationship-building. This is a common practice that values and prioritises efficiency over effectiveness.

Signposting has become such a difficult concept for me that the word itself is triggering. I have to reframe it in my mind as creating connections. I can think of many situations where someone has connected me to the right person or organisation at the right time. These connections are so valuable that I cannot bear to ruin them by calling them signposting.

To Understand All is to Forgive All

Essentially, a Quest becomes learning how to forgive a Society that has let you down. Not just to forgive but also to understand. The French have a saying: *tout comprendre c'est tout pardonner.* (*To understand all is to forgive all.*)

We try to understand so we can forgive. Once we can forgive we can let go.

Throughout this entire book I have referred to Society, but only referring to the shadow side of it. There are many positive aspects and people helping in Society. In my experience, these tend to be the exception rather than the rule. When I come across someone who engages with interest, responds in a timely and polite manner when doing their job, I notice because I am simply not used to it.

If you encounter anyone during your Quest that demonstrates a lack of interest, concern, or support, this is a clear indicator they are part of the problem of Society letting people down rather than part of the solution.

Whisper-Blowers

I want to take a moment to acknowledge and honour all the Allies in Society who go above and beyond the call of duty; who turn down the complacency of a career institutionalist trajectory; who value compassion, common sense, and commitment. Those who say *yes* to our calls of help instead of *no*. Those who find ways for us to sit at the table, and if that doesn't happen, give us a helping hand so we can stand on it. The Allies who understand that rules are guidelines and that sometimes the rules are simply wrong. I call them *whisper-blowers*. Whisper-blowers are different to whistle-blowers who essentially bring attention to illicit activity in a large, and sometimes public, organisation. The whisper-blowers keep an ear to the ground, and their eyes are truly open to the reality of Society letting us down. They find creative, hopeful ways to make changes from the inside of Society and assist those who are harmed by the societal organisations they work for. Although there is only a small paragraph for them in this book, it is written because of them. My hope is we can all encourage more Allies to do what you can, when you can, for all of us.

Meditating a Suitable Gift

As I get closer to finishing this book, I keep checking in with my daughter to see how she is feeling about it. Occasionally, I offer to read snippets to her, so I include her in the process. Some days she agrees, willing and able, and other times she declines still feeling tender from the trauma of Society letting her down.

I have just finished sharing with her a paragraph of this book and she pipes up to say, 'It reminds me of a poem we learned at school'.

'Really? What poem would that be'? I enquire.

'"Request to a Year". I can't remember the poet's name, but they were Australian,' she responds.

I am momentarily taken by surprise at her being taught an Australian poem in a Scottish school. With the majority of her education being in Scotland, the language of the land that birthed poets like Robert Burns and Sir Walter Scott.

'It wouldn't happen to be Judith Wright by any chance'? I offer randomly.

'Yes, that is it'! she exclaims.

I quickly go upstairs to my room to retrieve *Collected Poems*, by Judith Wright, that I have carried with me throughout my life. I open the first page, remembering how I received the book as a prize for winning best poem at my Australian high school. My English teacher had inscribed on the first page, '*I wish you wonderful reading adventures. Every good wish.*' Pieces of artwork I had made, when I was the same age as my daughter, are falling to the ground, having held the pages like portals for me to find my favourite poems. Holding this book feels significant, like I have travelled to my past, present, and future self all at the same time.

I find the poem and go back downstairs, and my daughter and I read it together.

REFLECTING QUESTIONS

» Why does Society see your situation differently than you do?

» What do you need to understand to be able to forgive so that you can let go?

» If you can understand, forgive, and let go what could you do with all your time, energy, and effort instead?

POTENTIAL ACTIONS

» Identify a time where you experienced the behaviour of a career institutionalist.

» Recall a time in which you displayed career institutionalist behaviours.

» Compare times when you were simply signposted versus when someone created connections for you.

» Create a series of steps that could move you toward forgiveness.

» As a source of motivation, make a plan with what you will do with your time and energy that can be redirected after your Quest.

Chapter 10

Part of the Solution or Part of the Problem?

It isn't what we say or think that defines us but what we do.

— **Jane Austen**

Solution

noun

an answer to a problem

THAT Person

I am a white, English-speaking, middle-class, university-educated woman. Part of why I felt compelled to accept our Quest was because I was privileged enough to have the means to do so. Not everyone is so fortunate.

I remember prior to that fateful day of 13 October, when I was there to pick the kids up after school, the palpable difference between the parents who felt comfortable enough to stand inside the schoolyard with everyone else to pick up their children, and the parents who would wait alone on the outer boundaries of the schoolyard. I would always try to stand and talk to those on the outside. I was really perplexed when they shared that they were too anxious to stand with the other parents. I now understand this for what it really was, an invisible line between the parents who were part of the problem of Society letting people down and those who were being let down. During our Quest I no longer wanted to stand in solidarity with those parents who were part of the problem.

My daughter had other children in her school share that her story was in fact their experience too. They shared with my daughter that they had informed their parents that the same thing had happened to them that had happened to her. Their parents chose not to accept a Quest. I accepted our Quest with their children in mind too.

Some of these are the same parents who were cherry-picked for the Parent / Head Teacher's Council. I remember earlier on our Quest I had reached out to invite one of these parents to our house, hopeful for some support, maybe even a sympathetic ear. Now, retrospectively, I see the situation for what it really was: the facade of support of solidarity for that is all they could offer and the only way they knew how to operate. I felt as empty as their offerings when they left. Sometimes I wonder if Society hadn't let us down would I have been like those parents and been part of the problem.

Even though we failed on our Quest, the fact we even tried, that I have written this book puts me on the path of hopefully being part of the solution in Society letting us down. Now I have the reputation of being *that* person. I can hear the eyes roll before I even enter the room. In some ways that makes my life easier. They know what they are up against now. Society knows that I will not accept them letting me, my family, or my community down. Society is wary of me, for I have let Society down.

When you have *that* reputation, word spreads quickly. I occasionally get phone calls from people all across the country who are considering accepting a Quest. There is a quiet network of Allies who connect those being swept under the carpet, and shunted into the corners of shame when Society lets them down. Somehow they get my name and number and reach out. Of course, I listen and I try to talk them out of a Quest by sharing all the things I have shared in this book.

But human nature is such that we think our story is different, and if they can just get the right information into the hands of the right people, they will make wise decisions. So naive.

We all make mistakes and are all guilty of not managing a situation as well as we perhaps wished. What matters is what we do after we acknowledge our mistakes and wrongdoings.

Managing Up

One of the techniques someone had identified that the head teacher had used was "managing up." Once this strategy was highlighted, I then witnessed it being used across multiple societal structures and agencies. Managing up means someone is not focusing their attention on what is happening to those they are responsible for because all their focus is on how they may be perceived by their superiors. They purposefully block information to ensure that key people are not alerted and policies and procedures not activated. If no one knows that Society is letting someone down, then no one can do anything about it, and more importantly, no one can be held accountable or liable. Ultimately, anyone managing up is part of the problem.

Pushing from the Top Down

To counteract managing up and be part of the solution rather than the problem, I learned how to push things from the top down. During the pandemic I learned this concept. Our organisation was looking for a building for our community food larder. There were plenty of vacant community buildings owned by the council, and I had been attending local meetings for the past six months, requesting to move the community food larder into one of them. Repeatedly I was told, 'No, this was not possible', but it was not the employees of the council's decision at these local community meetings to make.

What should have happened was my request should have been sent up the organisation to someone who was able to make that decision. The community larder could have ended there. Instead I bypassed all the employees, and went straight to the CEO of the council to ask him directly. Fortunately, he was able to make our request happen, and we were able to move the community food larder into the community centre. We pushed what we needed from the top down and as a result we were able to continue to feed hundreds of the most vulnerable in our community during the pandemic.

In our Quest, we were really fortunate when someone in the health service alerted the director of Education and Children Services, forcing them to acknowledge that Society had let us down and that key information from the bottom had not been passed up. Only then did our Quest start gaining momentum.

In a perfect world, people wouldn't feel the need to manage up or push from the top down. What would happen is if people needed help they would ask for it, be heard, and helped by someone willing to do so.

Society is a Narcissist

I remember someone once saying to me that Society is a narcissist. I had to look up the definition of *narcissist* as I wasn't familiar with it or convinced. The connection seemed overly dramatic. When I looked up the definition it sounded vaguely familiar and it took me a few days to work out why. The traits of narcissism paralleled the same findings of the Ombudsman investigation of Society.

- Failed to follow appropriate policies and procedures.
- Showed a lack of empathy or understanding in communications surrounding the impact of the incident and how our family had been treated.
- Made decisions based on personal opinion rather than professional assessment.
- A clear failure to involve our daughter and to take into account, openly and non-judgementally, her clearly stated views about the impact of what had happened on her.
- Significant failings in the way matters had been handled.

The Ombudsman upheld our complaint and verified Society had let us down. It was a six-month investigation conducted by a non-biased third party, which reviewed all the communication and documentation. This is why you document *everything*!

Words Unspoken and Meaningless Awards

The recommendation of the Ombudsman was that the head teacher, whose initial decision was the catalyst to all of this, apologise to my daughter. The head teacher refused. They refused to apologise to a student that the investigation proved they had been harmed under their care, on their watch, and who made decisions that caused our daughter further harm. Instead what my daughter received was a formal, cold response with no real feeling of accountability from the Education Department.

The school received a gold *United Nations Rights Respecting School* banner shortly after. The head teacher was promoted and moved onto other schools and continues to demonstrate poor judgement and decision-making that let children down. Before the head teacher left the school, her parting gift was to name an annual award after herself, to be given out at the end-of-year assembly. Not only did Society let my daughter down, it celebrated and thrived off her trauma.

I didn't change anything that I set out to change in our Quest—just as everyone warned and predicted. Yet, I can sleep peacefully at night knowing that I did everything humanly possible and in my power. My daughter witnessed me advocating for the life she wanted. There is much learning on the journey that shaped the future path we will walk. I am no longer naive.

REFLECTING QUESTIONS

» Who do you encounter that demonstrates a lack of interest, concern, or support in your Quest?

» How does identifying people who are part of the problem of Society letting people down rather than part of the solution inform your decision-making?

» Do the potential findings of your Quest have benefits for people who are more vulnerable, marginalised, or less privileged than you in Society?

» If you do not accept a Quest, does that make you feel part of the problem or part of the solution, and how does that make you feel?

Aftermath

More Power to Your Elbow

Silence hangs over us, but ... a different kind of silence, one that lets me breathe.

— **Chimamanda Ngozi Adichie,** *Purple Hibiscus*

More power to your elbow
Scottish saying
an expression of admiration for one's brave actions

Apology

I am sorry that this has happened to you. I hopefully don't mean reading this book but rather the reasons that called you to read it. We were one year through our Quest before someone actually said this to us.

'I am sorry this has happened to you'.

I am still moved by that memory.

A Grain of Sand

In the palm of my left hand, is a small pinch of sand, and I am trying my absolute hardest to count the individual grains. I am in my second year of primary school in Australia, and my teacher has just given us this task and I am determined not to let her down. She then holds out in front of us a small jar of sand, the one she had used to drop the tiny grains into our small, open, innocent palms. She asks us, 'How many grains of sand are in this jar'?

My eyes flit between the incalculable amount in the jar and the barely manageable amount in my hand, and I feel a slight panic start to prickle through me. Maths was never my strong point. No doubt some interesting debate ensued, and some braver children shouted some big numbers like ten million trillion gazillion!

Then our teacher said, 'How many grains of sand are there on your favourite beach'? I was dumbfounded. Being Australian, most children near a beach spend a great deal of time on it. We hop across the hot sand, squidge our toes into the wet cooling grains, but never had I considered the vastness of it.

'How many grains of sand are there in the whole world'? she questioned. My eight-year-old mind was blown, it was an overwhelming, impossible task. I could barely manage the pinch of sand in my hand, let alone comprehend every grain of sand in the world. I clearly remember sweeping the tiny, inconsequential grains from my hand onto the floor, watching them fall onto the scratchy carpet. I wiped my hands together to get the last ones off but some stuck to my hand. There are only two things I remember from that year at school. The boy that sat next to me peeing his pants and those grains of sand.

Society is overwhelming; like sand there is just so much of it — it sticks to us, falls from us, we traipse it into our lives unknowingly and sometimes, it is so embedded, it feels impossible to get it out of our lives and out the door where it belongs. How could we ever comprehend a concept so infinite when we feel so small and insignificant, like the tiniest grain of sand?

My hope is that the sands of time are turning, and the wind is changing direction. It is time to speak our stories of being let down by Society so that together we can write a new one.

Raise a Cup of Kindness Yet

My parting wish for you is that you find more power to your elbow. It doesn't surprise me that this saying originated out of Scotland, where people in the pub will punch you in the face, and then buy you a drink. I believe the saying originates from playing a bagpipe. This Scottish saying's imagery resonates with me. I see you standing with your hands on your hips defending this invisible boundary of where you end and Society begins, protecting your personal space with the sharp jut of your elbow. If you have any Scottish in you, I can also see it being a swift jab into someone's rib if required. It is about holding your ground, standing in your power, and knowing something even small can make a big impact.

May your power, and your elbow, serve you and Society well.

Acknowledgements

When writing this book, the similarities kept coming to me between being pregnant and birthing a book. Neither can be done well without the patience, engagement, nurturing, support, and expertise of others.

Naturally this book would not have been written if I had not been born by my parents, and the long line of those who came before them. For my life, I give gratitude and hope by trying to live well, I honour yours.

A bottomless well of gratitude to Paula Sarson, the book doula, who taught me how to be a better writer and always inspires me to be a better person.

Thank you to everyone who read the first draft and made it better: Auntie Jeannette, Jess, Mike, Morag, and especially Rachel for her 761 edits.

With wonder and awe I thank the generousity of Camilla and expertise of Latte for making this book breathe through design. A special mention to Lulu Morton for capturing the spirit of the book so beautifully in her illustration of the Emperor Moth.

Gratitude to Ally Apple who is always there to ask the right questions and help me find the answers.

I honour my teacher, Twobirds, who taught me that one can be reborn many times in a lifetime and whose teachings helped me survive.

To everyone at Platypus Publishing who made the road less travelled an empowering process.

Most of all I acknowledge you, the reader. You are the most important person for this book.

Printed in Great Britain
by Amazon

25628377R00076